My Hearts Ink
Imran Ali

Dear reader;

I see that you've purchased this book, for whatever reason it may be, I would just like to thank you. You're holding a part of me, a part of my life in your hands and now you have joined me in the next few chapters of my life. I'm about to take you on a journey - from the good, to the bad, to the great and I hope that you benefit from at least one thing written amongst these pages and when you reach the end of this book, I want you to understand that you are amazing and you deserve great things.

Contents:

The Loving

You're a garden full of roses,
one of the most
beautiful things I had
ever set my eyes on.
So delicate, every petal is
hugged against each
other to create
a masterpiece.
Only a hug with you
can recreate that masterpiece.

Our love is only
something
we can
understand
and that is what
makes our
love different.
Love isn't supposed
to be explained,
only felt.

You're a museum
of everything that
I want to see,
everything that I
want to feel,
everything I want
to have.

I don't know when it happened,
nor do I know how it happened,
but there is one thing for certain,
I am so glad to have fallen
in love with you.

Tell me about your day; tell me about how you were feeling. What happened on your journey to where you were going, what did you accomplish today? Did you laugh or find anything funny? Tell me so that we can laugh about them together. If you return home and I'm asleep, before you close your pretty eyes, whisper one thought that you had today into my ear, because I love the way you look at the world.

I remember him telling me once that the rain helped him sleep,
if only he knew that I prayed for rain every night just
so he could sleep peacefully. – J.I
I remember her telling me that romance had died and love
is something that she doesn't believe, if only she knew
that I prayed for love to flood her heart so that she's
at ease. – I.A

-Unconditional Love

I think that's the crazy thing, in a world full of fake love, the art of genuinely loving someone is rare. Every flower dies but it's going through a process, just like we do when we start to love. Starting with the seed, it's simply placed to grow, like two people being placed in each other's lives, learning about each other, growing with each other. Then the flower starts to bloom, emphasising the love that is starting to grow, loving life, everything is just beautiful. There will be thorns, showing the rough times there will be, one mishap doesn't mean it's the end. Of course the flower will die, but it doesn't reflect on the love that's dying. It is our time on this earth that is done, only to grow again when the seed is once again planted, but this time in the heavens, the place in which we'll meet again.

I've grown an interest in flowers ever
since my love has grown for you,
because just like how a flower
blooms, becomes greater and stronger,
you do too.

She started to tell me a hundred and one reasons
all explaining why she thinks she isn't pretty, but
then I stopped her mid way through and asked her
a simple question; 'what is the definition of pretty?'
She hesitated and said, 'Pretty is; being skinny,
not having glasses, no spots, having defined
cheekbones.' I stopped her and asked her;
'So who came up with this so called definition?'
She told me the world did. I said, the world is full
of people, people have opinions, so the 'definition'
that you have given me is merely just an opinion,
created by indoctrinated people of society.
The definition of pretty is endless. It's everything
and everyone. Not you, your friend, not anyone
is excluded from that definition.

I know you don't believe in love anymore but let me
pour my love into the broken parts of you so that
you'll have no choice but to feel like
you're being loved genuinely for the first time.

You're exactly the poem
that I've been searching to
read for my entire life.

The sunlight is all well and good,
but the sunlight wakes up everyone.
I'd rather have your lips
wake me up every morning,
nobody else gets the privilege
of your kisses.

You're my favourite chapter;
I don't have the heart to
turn the page.

They told me not to look at you,
I was confused, so I decided to look,
I instantly knew why they warned me,
because now I'm looking at you,
I can't seem to stop.

No words put together could create a dictionary definition
to describe how your lungs are filled with the purest
and sweetest air to exist, yet you would still be breathless
when I kiss you in the most passionate way possible.

It's 11:59pm
and I'm ready
to take on a
new day with
you.

It's 12:00am
and I start to
love you a
little more than
I did yesterday.

It's 12:01am
and I can't
seem to
comprehend
how you
made me fall
for you a little
harder...

...all in the
matter of
three minutes.

It was your eyes;
they stole all
my words away.
They brought back
all the feelings
I had caged away.

Wrapped in your arms, I started to melt;
now I'm ready to be stuck with you
in your sweet arms for the rest
of eternity.

I thought happy endings only existed in fairytales, who would have known that I had my own real life fairytale being told, my happy ending was saying goodnight to you after a long day of loving you.

I may not have superpowers like these people
do in the movies, nor do I have the ability
to take away every ounce of pain that you hold,
but I can love you at 3am in the morning
when no one else will, and maybe that's
where the magic lies and makes
it all worth it.

I don't want them to remember you, nor do I want your name falling off the edges of their lips. I want their memories of you to become nonexistent, their thoughts of you to vanish, almost as if you had never stepped one foot into their life, but the footprints you have left imprinted into their minds, I hope they were steps taken on sand, so the sea can wash them away, as if those steps weren't ever taken. I don't want them to notice the little things about you, let their memories of you dissolve into unknown parts of the world; let them be buried so deep so no one can ever find them again. They don't deserve to admire you the way I do, they really don't.

Connect the dots in the sky and
tell me if you can spell out your
name, because when I wished
upon a star that day, everything
changed.
-    *Star gazing*

When the walls begin to cave in and you start to feel suffocated with the world that surrounds you, remember that I will always be your safe place, your getaway and your home away from home.

Nothing haunts us like the things we don't say,
nothing haunts us like the things we stop ourselves
from expressing. I don't want to live my life
regretting that I never loved you the way you deserved
to be loved. So every day I remind you that my love
for you is inevitable, that you are precious and that you
mean everything to me.

A beautiful soul like yours deserves to
be written about and that is what I do
when you become the topic of my poetry.
You linger in every sentence, every word
and in every stanza, but you deserve more
than that. You deserve to be more than
just my poems, my muse and my topic,
you deserve novels written about you,
however the novels will be written
over the course of loving you in every
way humanly possible.

...and I looked at the moon that one night and noticed it was half covered by the darkness of the clouds. I gazed at the sky and noticed only half of it was filled with the stars. Although the moon and the stars were so far away, they still shone so bright, they made their presence evident. It reminded me of you, being so far away, half happy yet half covered with darkness, crying out for help. It was from that day I promised myself I will never let sadness touch you again, being half happy is not enough.

- *They liked darkness, so it was darkness they became.*

You dipped your toes into the darkness to see what it was like to be in my mind. I was afraid you didn't know how to swim, because with the thoughts that I get, it was almost certain I knew you were going to drown. I watched the light die in your eyes, so I wrote my love into a life ring to save you. The love, happiness and hope started to pump through your veins, as you appeared back up to the brim of darkness, you grasped for air and said; 'there is beauty in your struggle, I don't need saving, let me save you'. You held your breath and you confidently jumped back in. With your love, I can do the unthinkable. With every might and strength in your body, you became my saviour.

I wish there was an instruction manual, a guide, a set of rules that came with this, you know, me and you. This thing we got going on, this really big thing actually, anyways back to the point. I hate every argument that we have, every fight, every disagreement, I hate them all, if there were three things that I'd put at the top of the list of things that I hate, it would be arguing with you, all the emotions that come with it and the distance the arguments create. I envy the wind that touches your skin, I hate the floor that you walk upon, I dislike everything that is close to you when I'm not when we argue. Back to the first sentence, I wish there was an instruction manual, for when we argued I'd turn to that page and there would be a solution for me to read, understand and resolve the issue, but there isn't. So, I don't know how to handle every fight we're going to have, I won't know how to solve some of them either, but that doesn't mean that I'm going to give up. I will learn everything there is to know about you, every fine, hidden detail there is and I will create a book of my own, about you, about us and how every argument just grew us into better people and how they made us stronger.

-    *You are the authors of your love story*

The Misbehaving

I know it's been a long day, but I can guarantee you a good
night, good enough you won't want to say goodnight.
Forget about anything that is messing with your peace of mind.
If being bad feels this good then I will always commit
this crime, but what I'm asking you is;
can I love you a little harder tonight?

Let's get intellectually intimate;
I want to undress your thoughts
whilst I make love to your mind.
-Educate me in ways unimaginable

\-

Can I get a taste of you?
The taste will linger on my
tongue - you'll become my
favourite flavour.
You'll be my new addiction.
Good people, bad habits

Tell me that you want a real man,
I can make you feel like no man can,
the scratch marks on my back can
prove it.
-Love letters on my body.

You don't need to talk,
just let me love you in
every way possible.
Let your body become
one with mine; let our
bodies intertwine.
I'll make your body
call for me hours after
I'm done loving you.

Don't talk;
I want your tongue
to work for me
in other ways.

'Keep going'
what makes you think
that I'm ready to stop?
This isn't the kind
of loving that you're
used to, but don't worry,
this will be your new
favourite place to be.

People often drown in oceans;
I'm ready to drown in your pretty
little mess.

People tend to get lost in the woods;
I'm ready to get lost in between
your legs.

They told me to invest in the best
so tell me -
Shall we have a heart to heart?
Or shall we have a chest to chest?
-*Lets become fluent in the language of love*

I want to hear nothing but my name being echoed through
the hallway, repeatedly.
Allow me to show you how much
you really mean to me.

Leave a trail of kisses from my neck
right down to my chest and watch
the fire ignite. Let me leave marks
in places other people will never find.
- *Treasure on the map that only I'm able to find*

I put my finger over her lips and told her that's enough talking for the day, don't speak, lay back and allow me to show you how beautiful you really are, allow me to show you how you should be treated.

Every inch of your body could be up close to mine,
as close as it could be, yet I'd still want you
to be closer.
- *Close, but not close enough.*

Exhale,
I want to breathe
in every
wander of you.
-The air I breathe, I breathe for you.

...and when you thought this was it,
I loved you a little harder tonight.

I heard you would come back for more,
so I decided to go in like a savage like I'm
at war. I'll lift you up and put your back
to the wall, you don't have to talk,
I'm about to eat you alive like
I'm a cannibal.

I want you to write me love letters with
your nails on my back
and I can promise you I'll write back
to you with my tongue on your neck.
-    *To you, from me.*

Once our bodies intertwine,
I'll take you to a place
you didn't know existed.

Keep on going until you're shaking.
Let me touch your body - moan a little.
Let me touch your soul - moan a lot.

The Hurting

It's just one of those nights where my heart isn't at ease,
one of those nights where I wished for your company.
One of those nights where I can't stop thinking about you,
even though it's wrong of me to since you hurt me, but
it's just one of those nights where I could be at ease if you
were in my arms one last time, it's one of those nights where
I need you.

There is not a moment of the day where I stop thinking about being being by your side, making sure that you felt safe. To make you feel comforted and secure when I tell you that you're just mine and we have a stable future ahead of us. I wish I had done things so differently, now it feels so different from the first time. I wish I could take it back to the first time that I told you that I love you and how the meanings of those words haven't changed since the first night, I think about it all the time. I wish that I didn't have a thousand problems dragging me down whenever I wish to settle my heart. I wish I felt like I was enough for you.

-   *What is good enough? Is that really a thing?*

The late night conversations with you don't keep me up
at night anymore. The conversations that I have
with my broken conscious and inner demons do.
-    *Maybe it wasn't insomnia*

I still love you, but it hurts.
I don't have the heart to
blame you for what's happened,
so I tell everyone that I broke
my own heart loving you.

I can't seem to catch my stomach
when it drops so damn hard
at the thought of you with someone
that isn't me.

The person that filled me with so much life
is the same person that took it all away.
Where did all that disgustingly beautiful
love go?

-       *Disgustingly beautiful*

I write so that I can get my mind off of you,
the only problem is, I can't stop writing
about you.

I regret hurting you so much that it's taking you
a long time to get over me, but
loving you was the best decision I've ever made.

I hate the way you give others the same attention
that you give to me. There was me thinking that
I'm special to you, but yet again I was deceived.
-    *I was blinded by your 'love'*

Everyone knows that you lied to me
and they're all glad to see you gone,
but I can't help but think that right
next to you is where I belong,
but you were so messed up in your
mind, you failed to see what was
inside of mine.

I will tell you that I'm wrong and that I'm sorry
and everything is just my fault because my
heart can't handle losing you, even though
it's my heart that is breaking, not yours.

-How foolish of me, I just loved you too much.

I think it's time.
My heart is tired, it's had enough.
It's given up on everybody,
the only person that is left,
is me.

I don't understand why this always happens to me. My heart is already broken but I risked it all for you. For a split second I believed that if I let you in, you'd be my saviour and mend the damage. Why did I have to be so stupid to give you my all, almost expecting you to have some sort of ability to fix me or to change my perception of this cruel world and everyone that is in it. Why have you made me feel so confident in believing that if I let anyone else in, they'll just take a part of me and leave. That's what they've all done, taken parts that rightfully belong to me and have left me feeling empty. Now I'm not myself anymore. I'm just the parts of me that weren't good enough for you, that's why you left me behind. When will I ever be good enough?

You left me with nothing but that feeling of anxiety,
where I'll know you're holding hands with
someone better than I'll ever be. You left me with
nothing but that feeling of depression, where I'll know
 that you stole my heart but you gave yours to
someone else. You left me with nothing but that feeling
of loneliness, where I'll know that I gave up
everything for you but now you're gone, I'm left with
no one. You left me with no one but my own damn self.

- *You left me with nothing, but maybe that's all I needed.*

I'm not surprised when people break my trust or when they tell me that they've had enough; it's nothing new to me because people always leave. They promised they would never go and I thought okay they're genuine, your words I will believe. It's scary to think that one day they love you then the next day they don't, they told you hurting you would be the last thing they'd think of doing and they promised that they wouldn't. So tell me why my heart is hurting and why heartbreak is what I feel, being each others' motivation I thought that was the deal? Now my thoughts are everywhere and it's getting hard for me to speak. My mind is scarred and emotionally I'm becoming weak.

I'm sorry for all the times that I had hurt you whilst
I was hurting too. It's unfair and was never intentional.
You're someone that I love and hurting you would
be the last thing to cross my mind. I don't ever go out
of my way to make you feel like you're not good enough,
you are more than enough.
- *Unforgiving Apologies*

I loved you so much whilst
my heart was whole, now
you've broken it into little
pieces; I still manage to
love you a lot, with the
little that remains.

I undressed my heart -
it wasn't a pleasant sight.
Everything looked so
bruised, shattered and broken.
- *Internal Bruises*

Anytime I had felt pain, I would
come to you, you were my antidote.
Now that you've become the one
that is hurting me, how do I find
an antidote for you?

-When you opened the door to leave,
the antidote left with you

3:00am
laying on the grass,
looking at the stars,
wishing I wasn't laying
down here counting
all the problems in
my life. I'd rather
count the stars instead.

The Changing

It's okay to be selfish.
At the end of the day,
the thing that matters
the most is your own
happiness. At the end
of the day, the only
person who really stays
with you is yourself.

If you have to leave someone's life
in order to be happy, do it.
If they don't bring you any form
of happiness, then it will
damage you.

Whilst changing,
you may lose a few people
that you thought would never leave,
but remember that it's okay.
God is making room for better
things to enter your life.

- *In order to gain, you need to lose first.*

I can look you in the eyes and tell you that
I'm fine, but you'll be oblivious to the
fact that I'm dying on the inside,
but I promise you that one day I will
look you in the eyes and tell you that
I'm fine and I will actually mean it.

-But the eyes don't lie...

-

I was longing for someone to search for my cry
but it seemed like it was beyond this atmosphere.
I guess it's just me myself and I,
so I'll just find myself and fly myself out of here.

You are the sun that seeps through the
clouds on a grey, dull day.
You are that glimmer of hope.
- *The odd grey day is normal.*

Remember that anything that is beautiful,
people want to break, let in the right
people, because you are beautiful
and I am afraid.

The silence was getting too loud for me -
the thoughts in my head started eating me
alive. So I turned up the volume of success
and then I became unstoppable - sadness
couldn't touch me anymore.
-    *Why was the silence so loud?*

Tell yourself
that you deserve
every ounce of
happiness that
has ever
dropped onto
this earth.

Ask yourself; are your friends
or the people you associate with,
helping you to better yourself?
Or are they the reasons for your
downfall, the misguidance and
the reason why you are being
held back.
Finding good company is important.
-    *The blacksmith and the musk seller*

Focus on yourself.
Put yourself first,
besides, you know
what brings peace
to your own heart.
It belongs to you;
don't sit around
thinking you owe
another being a part
of your heart.
Own and embrace
what is rightfully
yours.

I want you to understand that your presence in this world is valuable and you are so precious. Life is too short - today is the day you tell yourself that you will never allow your past to catch up with you. You got this.

Shaking hands with my future,
saying farewell to the past,
but I keep memories in case
there's questions left to ask.

Forgive someone that has hurt your heart
so that you are finally able to find peace.
Remember that a person will not find
peace if they are going around breaking
the hearts of the innocent, whilst they
are on their quest of finding love.

- *Create peace with others first.*

Let go.
It's okay.
Remember how you
got through that fragment
of your life without this
person? You are able to
do that again, but this
time, even better.
Trust yourself.

You woke up and got out of bed today,
you haven't had the strength to do that
in a while, so the fact that you have done
so today, means that you are progressing.
Be proud of yourself, because that my love,
is bravery and the acceptance of change.
-    *One step closer to where you wish to be, congratulations.*

If you allow your past to tamper with
your future,
how do you expect to progress?

I had a story, but you're not in it anymore.
I pick myself up, when I'm beginning to fall.
It's not my fault that you blew it,
what you think is impossible,
I will do it.
-    *Some stories weren't meant to be completed.*

The moment that you've reached
your expectations, exceed the
expectations that you've already
met, because you are
capable of achieving so much more.

If you go through a downfall, it's okay.
Remind yourself that this is temporary
and it's not forever. It is a blessing,
you are being given a task to overcome,
to test your mental and emotional strength,
this is what you were waiting for right?
A chance to prove yourself that you are
not the same person you were before -
you are so much better.

Let today be the day you choose to
start working on becoming a better
version of yourself every day,
the day where you tell yourself that
you will never allow another person to
break you and that you are more than
enough for the right person.
Let today be the day where you make
some positive changes.

The New Beginning

I have learnt that,
the thing that is
the most important
is to put myself
first. I am my own
first priority.
-    *Sort out your priorities*

Thank you for being a part of a fraction of my life; you've helped me mould myself into a better person because now I've understood my actual worth. I've understood that you were holding me back because you were afraid to see me progress whilst you stayed behind. You made me understand that I made oceans of happiness for you, whilst I suffocated in your negativity and it should never have reached that point. I wish I could have helped you, I tried, but you have to help yourself first.

Understand it is okay to be broken.
Light seeps into the broken
parts of you and that is when
you find your hope. That
is when you start to feel better.

You may look at your scars and think that
they are a symbol of weakness, but it is not.
Be proud that you're still alive, breathing
and taking on another day with all your might.
Your next goal is to never let another scar
become imprinted onto your skin.
- *Thank you for not giving up.*

You have no control of the length
of your life, but what you do
have control over, is the depth of
it. You have the ability to bring
great meaning to your life,
go out there and find your
happiness.

The first rule of leading a good life;
Control your anger and
be abounding in love.

- *Self control is vital.*

-

When people start to disturb your
peace of mind and start to put a
threat towards your happiness,
don't fight back. Say nothing.
Ignore them - do not allow a single
part of them into your space.

- *You will not find peace with the peace breakers.*

Let go of everything that is holding you back. Take a second to go outside on a clear night, gaze into the sky, dream, believe and breathe.

I owe myself, my own damn self,
before I owe anything to
anybody else. I am mine,
before anyone else's.
- *Being selfish is allowed*

-

Surround yourself with people
that empower you, and if you
can't find those people,
become the person that has
the ability to empower others.
   -   *Don't feel threatened, feel empowered.*

Touch someone's soul and mind
before you touch their body,
that's when love becomes
unconditional.
Touch their
hearts first.

Just because you've done a few
bad things, that doesn't mean
you're a bad person. As long as
you accept that was the past
and those things were done by
the person you used to be and
you are a better version of yourself
now, understand you are a good
person, for taking action in
wanting to change.

You are the author of your own
book, the book of your life.
Make sure you take actions to
write a great one. Don't just
stop with one book, become
a saga.

Imagine your scars were wings,
fly away from all things negative,
and conquer your demons.

You've spent all your
life walking in shadows,
it's time to take that
one step out of it and
walk in the sunshine.

No mountain, sea or ocean
will ever be big enough
from stopping you from
reaching for your
happiness; it will never be
out of your reach. If it is
destined for you, then you
will get it.

- *Cross seas and deserts for yourself.*

Turn every negative situation into a positive one. Find the hidden blessing within the trial you are being put through. You are being given this trial to test your strength, ability and faith. You are also being given this ordeal so that you can learn, the next time you are put through a similar situation. You will know exactly how to overcome it.

The art of staying real
in a fake world is rare.
Become the greatest
artist.

- *Paint positive pictures*

You are a galaxy.
You have the ability
to make an empty
dark sky into
something
beautiful.

How great you are at what you do
can be inspiring to anyone.
Your ambition, your attitude,
your intelligence, everything is
empowering and that's the
thing that is attractive.

- *Reward yourself.*

Quotes and Poems to reflect on

Now I know not everyone is in love, or is hurting or
is in a relationship, so not all of the pieces of writing
you have read are able to reflect the situation you're in.
So here are a few quotes and poems for you to reflect on.

...and there is not a single thing in my past that I ever regret doing, because I have repented for the things that I have done, I have learnt and have become a better version of myself. If I had not done the things that I did, I wouldn't be the person that I am today. Yes, I will continue to make mistakes, that is guaranteed as it is human nature, but I will remember that every mistake is a lesson to learn from, a chance to gain knowledge on how to handle a situation better, if I am ever put through it again. It is also a chance for me to gain knowledge and share it with others so they don't have to go through all the struggles and hardships that I did. Every rejection that I get, every door that closes on me, I will never allow it to make me feel like I'm a failure. It is a chance for me to learn more about myself; new things are to be discovered every day, don't let one thing put you down, the things that you are stressed about today, may not be important a few months down the line, keep strong, you got this.

- *Chances upon chances*

I have family and friends I'm tired of running for,
I'm chasing shadows when I should be chasing dreams,
I'm friendly with the people that are undercover hating me,
I just want to go to sleep, but the grind is on my mind
so it's been disturbing the peace.

-   *Family doesn't have to be blood.*

In every situation you were put in, you had always picked to make others happy, but with every decision you made, a fragment of your happiness went. You were oblivious to the fact that you were draining yourself of your own happiness, whilst you created a sea of it for somebody else and now, now you wonder why you're emotionless and your heart feels heavy with emptiness.

- *Shades.*

You need to leave behind the weak minds, the ones who willingly choose not to open their eyes, the ones who hate happiness in other people's lives, the ones who go around telling lies, who make people feel sorry for them whilst making others cry, the ones who are insecure with themselves so they go around picking fights, the ones that mock you when you try, and always have an opinion on your life.

When someone has depression, it's not something
like a cold that will go away in a day or two. There
are constant waves of sadness, every wave with a
different speed and amount, the waves are filled with
sadness that floods their minds, convincing them that
there is a reason to be sad when they're genuinely happy,
there are thoughts in the back of their minds, full of
negativity, but they are not bad people, they are just
like everyone else. They feel the emotion of happiness
just like everyone else does, it's just hidden and it needs
to be found. Reassure them, tell them things will be
okay and their journey won't be a lonely one,
make them laugh, don't contribute to their sadness.

It feels like society has grabbed me by the throat and I'm suffocating, wondering why the people that make up society have become so blind, blindly hating, not knowing that it could be someone's last breath today. Imagine the last words you said to someone were negative, would you feel content with the things you said and left them with?

- A mistake I'm never making again.

If this is life, then why don't we just live it blind?
So we don't get to see the things that make us
hurt inside.

- *Count your blessings.*

You probably have an insecurity,
which was created by someone with no sense,
but I sense they have high levels of immaturity,
because of this you developed anxiety,
but trust me when I say you're beautiful there is no abnormality.
We have to start accepting diversity,
not judge each other based on ethnicity,
but promote highly on equality.
What's happened to humanity?
Even more so, what's wrong with our society,
trying to take away our identity?
Capitalist advertising constantly making us question our
masculinity or femininity,
which we all fall for because of our gullibility.
They do this intentionally,
marketing internationally,
now they think they have some sort of invincibility.
Broadcasting news which corrupts your mentality,
by people that are mediocrity,
this world is lacking normality.
They do this thing called agenda setting where
they pick what the media outlets show, this is
what you're letting?
What about the kids and people that are being abducted?
I think society needs to be reconstructed,
because it's all broken, wrong and corrupted.
-       *Will society ever be 'okay'?*

To my people of colour,
there is too much hate in this world for us to be against each other.
Yes, our histories are completely different and there are things that
our countries have done wrong, things so wrong that they are almost
absolutely unforgiveable, but we can't let this affect our relationships
today. They are already trying to take away our cultures, the next
generations don't know how to speak their mother tongue, the
traditional dressing is becoming out dated for them, our cultural
foods are not being embraced and eaten because of these fast food
chains and healthy diets these celebrities endorse, we can't let this
happen. There have been wars, deaths, sadness and clashes between
countries, but being a person of colour and putting down another
person of colour is not what we need today. It is time for us to make
a stand, time for us to prove a point, that although our cultures are
different, although there have always been problems in the past,
we will empower each other today. Brown skin, yet we all bleed the same.

The Ending

You've made it to the end of my book; you have a part of my life in the palm of your hands. Too many times in the course of my life, I have given parts of myself to people that didn't deserve to even know a fragment of what happens in it or what feelings I feel, but this? Handing over this part of my life to you, containing feelings and emotions that I have felt at least once in my life, I am doing this confidently and I am certain that this is the best part of me that I am handing over to you.

To every person that has ever entered my life, whether you brought me complete happiness or absolute sadness, I am here to thank you for what you did. To the people that have always believed in me and to the people that have always wanted to break me, to the people that have left me and to the people that have stayed, to the people that I love but are now in the heavens above, thank you, so much for doing whatever you did, because without you, I wouldn't be here, writing this book today.

Whatever emotions you must be feeling right now as you read this, I hope happiness enters your life and remains there, that sadness doesn't touch you and if you ever feel hurt? Know that you are absolutely strong enough to recover from it. Placing my hand on my heart as these words are entering your mind, I really do thank you for taking the time to reach the end of this book. May love always linger in your heart, may happiness always project from your eyes, I am writing to you, with my hearts ink.

- *A love letter from me to you.*

-

A special thank you,
To the woman who is the main reason why this book was written and published. Without her, this book wouldn't be in your hands at this very moment, so if there were to be anyone you should thank, it should be her.

-For that, I am forever in debt to you.
-J.I

Printed in Poland
by Amazon Fulfillment
Poland Sp. z o.o., Wrocław